Nobody Understands Me but My Therapist

NORMALIZING THERAPY WHEN DEPRESSION, ANXIETY & LIMITING BELIEFS ARE REAL

Kelsey Brewster

Paperback ISBN: 978-1-63616-049-8

eBook ISBN: 978-1-63616-050-4

Published by Opportune Independent Publishing Company

For permission requests, write to the publisher, addressed "Attention: Permissions Coordinator" to the address below.

Email: Info@opportunepublishing.com

Address: 113 N. Live Oak Street
Houston, TX 77003

DEDICATION

This book is dedicated to all the black mental health professionals who are effectively creating a safe space for black women like myself who are committed to living healthier lives. Your dedication to your practice and the well-being of our community does not go unnoticed. You are a part of the change to give people light and hope, and for that you are much appreciated. Special thank you to you "my therapist". Your impact, knowledge and professionalism is unmatched. I thank you for being a part of my journey. I believe it was destined.

CONTENTS

ACKNOWLEDGMENTS

There are no words that can describe this moment, this accomplishment. I must give praises to God for blessing me with the vision and foresight to write and publish this book. Leading and guiding me even in those moments where I pushed back on making this a reality. I want to thank my family and friends for all your love and support throughout the years. I have embarked on multiple endeavors throughout my life, and there has always been a core group of people who have remained by my side. (You know who you are) And although I decided to write this book in private with only very few knowing about it, I know that their love and support were with me through and through. I want to thank my mother for being my first example for writing. You may deny it, mama, but you are a great writer and an inspiration. I love you.

I must thank my book coach, Nikkie Pryce, for guiding me throughout this process and spiritually advising me. Our discussions brought light and depth to this process. Thank you for being authentic and for holding me accountable.

INTRODUCTION
WHY THIS BOOK?

"It's ok to feel delicate sometimes. Real beauty is in the fragility of your petals. A rose that never wilts isn't a rose at all"

—Crystal Woods

When I was younger, starting in grade in school, I developed a love for writing. It all started through school assignments, of course. But that love quickly expanded after a cute, short poem about the "Sun" that I wrote was published in a book highlighting young writers of the South. From there, I began to write often during those early years, there were more poems, short stories, and then eventually speeches. I had this hidden dream of becoming a published book author even during the periods where I didn't write as often or at all. Writing was an escape yet a way for me to articulate my thoughts privately because I was never big on being front and center all the time. However, here I am with my very first published book sharing my journey with mental health, how I found support through therapy and why I believe you can too. From aspiring to implode the world with imaginary literature to baring the state of my reality.

Life can be beautiful, smooth, rosy, and amazing. Yet, it has unpleasant sides as well. Sometimes, when we are faced with mountains that look insurmountable, all we need to do is open up and seek help, rather than assume everything is fine and drown in the sea of frustration.

Do you ever find yourself in constant emotional pain? Have you ever considered seeking out clinical talk therapy? Are you embarrassed or ashamed to seek help? Do you feel uncomfortable when discussing your feelings, traumas, and/or behaviors? What's your perception of mental health and therapy? I believe that our perceptions, environment, culture, and lack of resources have become the premise for therapy not being a source of healing and treatment, particularly in African-American society. African Americans are typically more concerned about therapy's stigmas and are more likely to feel ashamed for even considering mental health treatment. I get it! Mental health providers don't always look like us, nor do they understand our needs. There is a significant number of people of color seeking help but are often discouraged when they cannot obtain a culturally proficient provider to provide the care they need.

When writing this book, drafting the title, I kept trying to run away from the word "Normalize", which you've probably heard more often over the last couple of years. In today's culture, especially with the dominance of social media, words can oftentimes become a trend. There are so many words and catchphrases that some people are either trying to cancel ("cancel culture") or hold on to for dear life. So when I thought about what I wanted my message to be for this book and what I wanted readers to walk away with, it all kept leading me back to me promoting normalcy. When something has extreme stigmatized beliefs surrounding it, it is deemed to not be normal. And for decades, therapy has been linked with so many.

I decided to write this book in hopes that it will help someone else; let them know that it's okay to not be okay, yet you don't have to remain that way. That as much as you talk about the up and rosy side of life, it's okay to discuss the down and thorny side too. And that seeking therapy to better your mental health is nothing to be ashamed of, nor should you allow the opinions of others to stop you. Trust me, I understand. I was once that person. If you look at me from the outside, you may suppose I don't have any problems, and I may be one of the happiest people on earth. But the truth is, I'm human; just like anybody—we're bound to have problems, great or small.

It's important to note that this book wasn't written to publicly bash anyone in my life for not understanding me but to raise my hand and let others—especially those who look like me—know that therapy helps, and it's vital. So as a corporate professional, I completely understand the importance of writing to inform, but I'm also a black woman of the south who loves a good girl chat session and even more so over a good meal. So, understand that not only will I use my words to inform you but also use my voice so that you can hear yours. So that you can see yourself through my journey, so that you'll be able to relate. Therefore, you will be able to take action. I want to let you know that if you are battling depression, anxiety, or both, it's a battle that's bigger than just venting to a loved one or just letting yourself heal with time. (I personally tried that, and it did not work!) And, it's way beyond your power to handle it alone. But, hey! It doesn't mean you're crazy! It means that there are things you need to sort out and unpack to keep your mental sanity. And, if you're not suffering from depression, anxiety, or any other mental illness, you too can find therapy to be extremely beneficial for your life.

Also, I hope that this book continues to create awareness about the importance of mental health, especially in the African American community in order to break stigmas, and most importantly, save lives. The truth is, cost and limiting resources are attributed to therapy not being a sought-after method for mental health illnesses for people of color. Yet, I am optimistic that the more we talk about it, the more resources will be created to give many people the privilege to apply this method to their lives.

This book seeks to help women of color end the stigmas that accompany mental health and therapy, particularly in the African American community, and to provide hope and encouragement. This is for those women of color who are trying to have it all together, especially because everyone thinks they should. The selfless who are fond of reaching out to others when they're down yet refuse to ask for support in their own difficult time. And those who know something is wrong internally, but they neither identify what it is nor how to fix it. I believe I represent all those who can identify with these characteristics and more.

The Centers for Disease, Control and Prevention

(CDC) speculate that mental health is a vital aspect of our overall health and well-being. It accounts for our emotional, psychological, and social makeup[1]. Sadly, this subject matter had been taboo in the African American community for a long time. But the good news is, there is more conversation surrounding this topic today. And people in the community are becoming more comfortable discussing this vital topic to help erase the stigma.

Today, prominent African-Americans like Taraji P. Henson are using their platforms to tell their stories, opening the dialogue, and providing resources to our community. When I see people like Taraji, who are under intense scrutiny every day, stepping forward for the benefit of the community, it gives me—the average working woman, the courage to replicate the good work and make my own societal impact. The truth is, African-Americans are more likely to have serious psychological distress than Whites. And that's one of the reasons mental health in the African-American community should be taken more seriously.

Research has it that there are roughly two hundred classified forms of mental illness. Also, nearly one in five adult Americans will have a diagnosable mental health

_____

1 Cdc.gov/mentalhealth,index.htmss

condition in any given year. Some of these common disorders are depression, bipolar disorder, dementia, schizophrenia, and anxiety disorders. In truth, I wouldn't claim that I'm qualified to educate anyone on these disorders from a clinical lense. I can only speak from my personal experiences and research.

Our first impulses are usually to suppress and move on from those things that emotionally scare us. We must break this habit, we must recognize that it's unhealthy for us, both physically and mentally.

Perhaps you have a loved one struggling with a similar challenge who could benefit from therapy, and you don't know how to help or encourage them to take actions toward receiving the needed assistance. I hope this book assists you as well, not only on how to help them but also by providing you with some encouragement to not give up on them. One thing is for sure, having a loving, faithful support system is just as crucial as therapy is for someone with mental and emotional struggles. Don't let the previous failed attempts stop you from supporting, loving, and believing in your loved ones. You must understand that their battle is probably bigger than you could imagine. And, trust me, it's an empty feeling when someone who says they have your back gives up on you.

In subsequent chapters, I will discuss my journey at a glance and how I've benefited from therapy. I'll break down the key areas that I struggled with and how therapy helped me identify and deal with them. Also, I'll share some insight and revelations that can help you and lead you to practical ways to seek therapy. I'm still a working progress, but I felt the need to share my voice, turning my emotional mess into a message. So here goes...

PART 1:
OBLIVIOUS & LOVING IT

CHAPTER 1
THE WOUNDS OF INDESCRIBABLE PAIN

"Turn your wounds into wisdom."
—Oprah Winfrey

I would never have thought I would get to a place in life where I would feel lost and without hope. You hear people say this, and you may honestly not know what that means or even how that feels. In life, everyone will go through storms, either financially, emotionally, psychologically or have a challenge in their health. I can honestly say I felt completely lost with no direction at one point in time. I was confused as to what makes me happy and simply who Kelsey was. Carrying an abundance of confusion, being unfulfilled nor satisfied has been known to create emotional affliction. Can you relate to that feeling? Have you been in a space where so many things such as rejection, trauma, grief or loss of identity have caused you to question your complete existence? And you find yourself trying to escape the feeling by any means necessary.

Well, once upon a time, I walked into a hospital to get help. I never imagined myself having to do that unless something was physically wrong with me, not mentally. But I had reached my breaking point, so I felt that it was the best thing to do at that time. I knew what was going on; I knew how I was feeling and knew I didn't want to any longer. I simply wanted to get away and be in some type of isolation. Deep down, I feared where my emotions would lead me. I had reached a point where I was checking out on life. After five days in treatment, I walked out of that hospital, still somewhat feeling lost, feeling anxious about what I should do next, and also with a major depressive disorder/ anxiety diagnosis. But, I was hopeful.

In reality, I didn't know what to expect when I walked into that hospital. People who have not experienced such an environment can only relate to either what they see or hear from the media or what they hear from someone who has been there. Indeed, I was anxious and apprehensive! Nonetheless, I adapted and got comfortable around the second day. From the scheduled medication to the group therapy sessions and connecting with the other women, I actually felt good about my decision to go there. Surprisingly, part of me didn't want to leave when it was time because I was apprehensive about whether I would be in a better space, and admittedly I wanted to stay in that bubble a little while longer.

Unloading pain is probably the most uncomfortable part of healing. When I decided to write this book, the part I dreaded writing about the most was my pain. But I had to ask myself, "How can you write to help others and not talk about the pain that led you to this very point?" When God began to speak to me about this book, I was fearful, resistant and sometimes, I even cried because I didn't understand why God wanted me to expose myself. The thing is, I didn't want to talk about my pain because I was afraid of so many things. One of the things I wanted to avoid was judgment.

All my life, I have always cared about what others thought of me, and it's been a negative crutch that I am still dealing with in therapy today. I wasn't just worried about what my family and friends would say; I cared about what strangers would label me as. Sounds crazy, right? Like, have you ever been so overwhelmed about the potential judgment you may receive from complete strangers? Worrying about what a complete stranger would think of me should be the least of my worries during writing this book, right? But it was. I felt like writing this book and discussing the not-so-good moments would in some way have me publicly standing in front of the judge and jury to decide the fate of who Kelsey is and how I should feel about myself. Hmmm, WOW! But let's be honest, we all have passed judgment at some points in our life. This is one revelation that I work to remember when consumed by what others may say or think. Not only that, but also not simply considering the opinions of other people. That's a whole other topic of discussion within itself. We will discuss it further along in the book.

Shame played a huge role in my reasoning for not wanting to share the difficult points of my journey. In my mind, the things I had experienced I shouldn't have even experienced at that point in my life. Nor should I have experienced it because I should have been wise enough, equipped with the knowledge and a sound mind to always make good decisions. Well, at least that's what I thought. That was how I viewed myself for so long, frequently forgetting that I was human and bound to make mistakes. Nevertheless, the shame I felt contributed greatly to my depression and ultimately caused me even more pain. Yes, sometimes our pain is self-inflicted and even harder to overcome.

And the last reason that would have held me back from discussing my pain would be privacy. I've never been big on sharing all my personal business. And I still to this day stand firm on that mentality. However, it was my privacy mentality that was holding me back when it came to seeking help through therapy, so I can't allow that same mentality to hinder me from helping others through this book. Now I see that it's okay to pick and choose what to share, how to share it and who to share it with. I've come to understand that it's the purpose of the message that's the importance. Like my book coach, Nikkie Pryce, explained to me, "it's not solely about the story but the lessons". So, when we go out to share things, I believe it's important to ask the question, "is there a purpose?" If so, what is that purpose? Is there a reason why this information is disclosed? What do you hope to get out of sharing this personal information? For me, sharing my journey and pain through this book is for two reasons; to use my God-given gift (1 Peter 4: 10-11) of writing and to help others overcome and understand mental health from my personal perceptive and why therapy is so important.

THE BREAKING POINT

So, what was it that led me to the point where I felt the need to be in isolation and seek medical attention? Most people believe that life is worth living even when it's difficult. Well, as true as that statement is, there was a time when I didn't believe that.

Suicide is a global crisis that continues to rise year after year. People who you may least suspect have had suicidal thoughts. And I wouldn't have thought that I'd ever have suicidal thoughts myself. But, it was my reality, and I own it. I began nursing these thoughts a few years ago after I left an emotionally and sexually abusive situation. My initial anger (after removing myself from that situation) was instantly followed with guilt and shame. But it wasn't just because of all that I endured, but also me going above and beyond to hold on to that situation before walking away. The fact is that situation only left me angry with myself. Asking myself repeatedly, how could you put yourself in such a situation that would cause you to end up extremely broken? Why did you ignore the red flags? Because sis, they were definitely there. You should have walked away sooner than you did! You should not have gone above and beyond to hold on to something nowhere near being worth it. All these questions and thoughts consumed me and pushed me into a state of darkness.

The truth of the matter is I was suffering long before that situation. I felt completely alone, extremely sad, and my self-esteem was at an all-time low. In truth, I've always dealt with low self-esteem. I had little to no confidence in myself at most times and sometimes didn't know how to approach situations, whether big or small. To some who know me, that may come as a shock because I may project confidence at times, but deep down, it was a real struggle. I wouldn't always like who I saw in the mirror and constantly put myself down whether in private or to others. No matter how many compliments I would get, it never seemed to matter because deep down, I just didn't love myself wholly as I should have. So, each time I questioned myself regarding that situation, I felt guilty for everything that happened, everything I did and everything I did not do. So with all of that, I could neither forgive myself nor show myself some love or grace.

When I started having suicidal thoughts, they started as ideations of not hurting myself directly but were more of me having visions of getting into an accident. I can remember being in the car driving many times, visualizing myself getting into a fatal car crash. I ultimately didn't want to be responsible for my own death, but I imagined it. Then later down the line, I started reaching for pills. The first time I poured out about thirty pills on the counter and just cried. By this time, my dark moments seemed to be getting darker and darker. I truly didn't dare to do it but wanted to end the pain somehow. Then the last time, I did take some of those pills and the next morning was angry that I woke up. It's painful to type the words, but I'm hoping my honesty will help someone else. The reality is I didn't really want to end my life. I just wanted to end the pain, cease the thoughts and not continue to face my internal battles.

Most people view suicide as a selfish act. But I must admit that I thought that everyone would be better off during those times. I genuinely thought because I couldn't give everyone around me a stronger version of me that they would be better off without me. Of course, now I know that was the furthest from the truth. I know that my presence in my family and friends' life is unmatched and irreplaceable. Yes, it was important for me to get well and be mentally strong, but I didn't understand that I didn't always have to have it all together.

If you or someone you know has dealt with suicidal

thoughts and attempts, you should know that it all stems from some indescribable pain. Pain that's yearning to be released and no longer be a burden. Understand that those suicidal thoughts come from a place of feeling like you are on the complete edge and with nowhere else to go. So, if you have never been at any of those points, try not to judge what you can't relate to.

I found myself at a place where I was carrying so many burdens. And eventually, those burdens took on a life of themselves, forming into depression and anxiety. Whew, Depression! Depression was one of those words I heard but never really paid attention to or even took the time to fully understand the depths of it. Anxiety as well, a word I was familiar with but honestly never really understood its seriousness and how it can become a daily battle to overcome.

CHAPTER 2
STUCK ON THE INSIDE

"To ignore or wish our wounds away is to simply create an environment for them to fester and become infected. Untreated wounds make us sick."

—Unknown

Have you ever done something and constantly questioned your reasons for doing it? What about the words you speak? Have you ever said something or used a negative tone with someone for no reason? It's adherent that sometimes, as humans, (emphasis on sometimes) we do things and do not know why. However, learning to understand why we do what we do or say what we say is at the core of working to overcome pain or hurt. Not to steer away from responsibility, however, when you've experienced trauma and do not deal with it, at times, that trauma transforms us in some areas where we then become unrecognizable. I won't deny that there were moments where I did not recognize myself but more so how the effects of repressed feelings were showing outwardly. Those repressed feelings started to show up at times where I needed to remain calm. Times where others may have needed my strength. But in the moments where I did not overact, I learned how to mask it all. I got really good at concealing my feelings only showing an acceptable face to others. For decades and even probably before then, black women have accepted the notion that no matter what is going on, no matter how bad things may seem, hold your head up and push on. Black women have for a very long time subscribed to the ideology that asking for help was wrong. Especially in regards to emotions. That the only time to cry or show any emotional anguish was done privately. And that it's not right to let anyone, let alone the world, know you are not okay.

After my situation, I felt broken, yet I was still going through the motions. Although my days were going by, my past was lingering in the shadows. I thought that if I avoided my pain, it would eventually go away on its own. But I was obviously wrong. The more I buried my pain, the more it would resurface, and it always seemed to be at the wrong time. Before I knew it, all my pain was catching up to me, and I didn't know how to control it.

There was a time where sleep was the only remedy I had for my pain. Sometimes, I'd go to work, return, and just go straight to bed. As I look back now, I know it was at this point I should have sought out therapy. But therapy was the farthest thing from my mind. So what did I do? I suppressed it and pushed forward.

I tried to escape from my pain by starting a travel business that eventually took my evenings after work. Traveling became a passion of mine a few years before this, and so I thought, why not turn it into a business? Although I was blessed with a full-time corporate career, I always looked for additional income streams. To the outside world, I was becoming a travel agent to help others travel more and generate income, but for me, it was also that I needed a good distraction. It obviously wasn't a bad distraction; it kept me busy and focused. Before I knew it, being a travel agent had my full attention, and I started to think about my pain a little less each day. Becoming a travel agent brought me much success. I met new people and was tapping into my creative side in marketing my business. Within a few months, I was fully committed to this new journey and saw so much future in it.

Every day that I got up to face the world, I'd wear

a "mask" so that people wouldn't know that I had many days where I was struggling. I remember a day I was at work; as I got off the elevator, a coworker who I knew well complimented me on my then weight loss. "Girl, you lost so much weight. You look good". I said thank you, but I knew I wasn't on any diet or workout plan. I just wasn't eating. Now I understand that this is what clinical professionals define as a depressive episode. It amazes me how we can go through these low points in life and cover them so well that nobody knows. But no matter how much I suppressed it or distracted myself, the fact is, that situation and so much more was haunting me.

Releasing what's on the inside that's causing pain and anxiety is by far the hardest step to do on the road to healing, but it's the first and greatest step of them all. Like I've said before, I was so accustomed to bottling things up that I really didn't know any other way to deal with things. I was harboring so much from the past that sometimes it was difficult to be in the present moments. There have been many times when I was amongst others seemingly having a good time (and probably really was) but was also stuck on something I probably had no control over to change. Quiet naturally, we detest the painful, ugly parts of our lives and prefer never to revisit or discuss them ever again. One of the very first things I did after my trauma was simply move on. As if it didn't happen or that it was simply no big deal. Why is that when something bad happens, we naturally react by not reacting? I can recall speaking to the one person I told a little after it happened, one of my very close friends, and I remember her saying as much as she could but I could tell that she really didn't know exactly what to say. But she told me I needed to speak with someone and let me know this more than once. She even pushed me by taking action and going herself for those things she dealt with.

My first thoughts right after that moment were to naturally forget it, but in all actuality, I never forgot it. And that was apparent through those random moments of darkness that I would have. Even still, to this very day, it's a moment that frequently pops in my head. When you are in denial about a traumatic experience you want to forget it and convince yourself that it didn't happen. Looking back now, I realize that by holding on to it, all I was doing was building resentfulness, anger, bitterness accompanied with self-pity. As women, we go through so much yet always find a way to push on. I found myself in a full-on marathon trying to run away from this pain and anger, but when I stumbled would be reminded of all that I was holding on to. I continued to hold onto this pain; it only increased my burdens which again turned into depression and anxiety.

Visions of a moment where you are trying to understand why, the image of a man with his arms pinned to his side to apply extra weight to you and remembering how tired you became trying to break free. A moment where the self worth you do have slowly exits your body and soul, leaving you feeling empty and breathless. It's literally a recurring nightmare that's a glimpse of my past. A reality I no longer want to be bound to. Realizing that those images may not ever go away, the resentment you may fester in your soul forever or having the constant internal conversation with yourself trying to figure out what you could have done to prevent it from happening. Over and over again in your mind trying to make sense of it all.

So distracting myself from the internal battles seemed to be the best option. Simply having the feelings and thoughts that things will not get better. At some points, I became discouraged more and more that I felt I'd never be able to shake it off. I started to believe that that dark moment would turn my life completely dark forever, holding me hostage until I'm no longer breathing. Thinking my soul would never be at rest or at peace. This was clear evidence of me living through my limiting beliefs.

REDEFINING TRAUMA

Trauma is real! The craziest part about trauma is that we don't always know that we have experienced it. Disclaimer...Therapy will in fact, redefine words for you. You may think you know the meaning and fully understand the words you hear all the time. But just knowing the definition does not always provide the clarity to know how you've personally encountered such words. When it came to trauma, I only had it limited to certain things and events. However, trauma can be a variation of experiences, such as a serious injury, natural disaster (hurricane, flood or earthquake), sudden or unexpected death of a loved one, or community violence (police brutality, mugging, assault). When I would reflect on my sexual abuse experience, I never defined it as trauma or traumatic. I think I created trauma to look a certain way in my mind, and at the beginning, it didn't look like my experience. As bad as it was, I always seemed to downplay it as I compared it to other's experiences. For instance, dismissing it because there wasn't perhaps a gun pointed at my head or that the person wasn't a complete stranger.

While most people often saw me smiling, laughing, and flourishing, I was having difficulty accepting and expressing painful feelings and emotions. While carrying my burdens, I ensured that I cared for others the same as always. However, at the very same time, I was feeling unworthy of that same love. Many people saw me achieving success with my travel business however, I was also feeling undeserving of it all. Saw me putting in the time, long hours to operate my business, but in reality, I was trying to distract myself until the memories, pain and anguish all went away. Depression, anxiety, or the aftermath of trauma don't always look how it does in our minds. The external world does not always match what is going on in the internal world.

Guilt had settled and made a home in my soul. When you are wounded with trauma, it affects your soul with feelings of an enormous amount of guilt and shame. For a while there, I was trying various ways to ignore the pain and guilt. My limiting belief that it was all my fault was living wild and free on the outside, becoming a reflection of my most dominant thoughts. Developing into uneasiness and unhappiness, therefore, holding my faith and ability to break away from that belief.

I now understand that sometimes we don't always know how traumatic something we experienced truly is until we actually talk about it. Sometimes, it takes other people's reactions to let us know that what we experienced was indeed traumatic. When you come out of a toxic or traumatic situation where something precious as your ability to say no is taken from you, it can leave you feeling empty and lost. By my fifth or sixth session with my therapist, I had finally found the courage and strength to recant my sexual abuse experience fully. For a long time, I was extremely confused about the situation and wasn't sure if what happened, happened. Now, looking back, I realized the denial I was in at that time. For a long time, I convinced myself that it was no big deal and that I was okay. I knew that afterward I was angry and partly confused. But finally, after recanting detail by detail with my therapist, there was finally some relief. For two reasons, my therapist confirmed that it was indeed a traumatic experience (what I thought happened, happened), and I finally stated every detail of what happened out loud. Therapy has helped me process that moment, work to release ownership and set my intentions on internal peace.

CHAPTER 3
MIND PLAYING TRICKS

"We see things the way our minds have instructed our eyes to see."

—**Muhammad Yunus**

We become a reflection of our most dominant thoughts. A caption from James Allen strongly resonates that says, "You are today where your thoughts have brought you, you will be tomorrow where your thoughts take you." The reality of anxiety is that you can be confident, seem happy and be a complete mess on the inside. I believed I had an image to uphold, and being vulnerable wasn't part of it. That became my defensive mechanism, and it definitely made it hard for anyone around me to really help me.

After my release from the hospital, I found comfort in listening to audiobooks and motivational YouTube videos. I realized that I had to cut down on the music to hear the more positive dialogues. Don't get me wrong. I'm not saying that music influenced me negatively, but it was not nurturing my mind the way I needed .

One of the books that helped me navigate the valleys of anxiety was Shook One: Anxiety Playing Tricks on Me[2] by Charlamagne tha God. The book's title was inspired by a song from the hip hop group, Mobb Deep's 1995 song "Shook Ones".

In his book, Charlamagne reveals the blueprints that enabled him to break free from the shackles of fear and anxiety or, more so, how to manage them. He described how the grip of anxiety took over him from his childhood days till when he became an adult. If you are a fan of him, I'm sure you're aware of his mental health advocacy.

This black man consistently speaks on the benefits of therapy, encouraging everyone, especially people of the same color, to seek therapy no matter what they are dealing with. He clearly stated how life became so overwhelming that he could no longer run from seeking out help. He details how therapy assisted him in effectively managing his anxiety that stems from childhood that crept into his life as an adult man.

---

2 https://www.amazon.com/Shook-One-Anxiety-Playing-Tricks/dp/1501193252

In the book, he showed how in situations his mind would go into an overdrive of thoughts and ideations that would cause panic attacks.

His story really made me evaluate my journey and how anxiety affects me. For me, I've always been an over-thinker. It became a concern as I grew older as I tried to deal with life's peaks and valleys. Sometimes, it was debilitating because I eventually became so consumed by my thoughts. Have you ever just laid in bed wishing your mind would shut off so you could rest? That was how I felt, both day and night. This led me to think that the instability of my mind would make me make decisions that would make or break me.

I was so focused on things that hadn't happened, for example, marriage and children, a different job, and an increased salary, that I lost sight of the things that had already happened in my life. Although, at a time, I was in a committed relationship where marriage was understood to be the goal, I still had anxiety about it because I honestly wasn't confident enough in it happening for me. I had convinced myself that by being over 30, my time was running short. I was also letting the opinions of family and friends cloud my judgment. You know people may mean well sometimes, but the ever so often questions or comments like "when are you going to have kids?" Or "don't wait until you get too old" start to get to you. But when you find yourself looking around still single and with no kids, it does lead you to feel like something just may be wrong with you.

I got so tired of walking in fear, but I honestly didn't know how not to, and it scared me. Quite naturally, we all get anxious about the future. Anxiety will make you question everything and everyone, sending you down a rabbit hole of thoughts. It got so bad for me; that I felt like I was losing my mind. And the hardest thing to do was shut my mind down.

But being over 30, I became consumed with the ticking of my biological clock. This was a major contributing factor to my depressive and anxious state. Actually, when I turned 30, it didn't hit me right away, but as I attended funerals more often, I began to adjust my lens to how life really looked.

It leads you to not really care about the things you've accomplished and experienced in life from a positive standpoint but rather makes you focus on who is around you. And then the big questions start to roll in, making you obsessive, "what's wrong with me?" Even when it seems like all was in my path, and I could see it, there was still uncertainty and fear that it wouldn't actually happen.

I've heard people say that marriage and kids aren't all

that life is made out to be just because they've may had some regret. But for me, I didn't care about their views or personal experiences. All I was thinking about was having a family and building a legacy that my parents could witness.

DEALING WITH GRIEF AND GUILT

Life and death are two major aspects of this thing we call evolution. Death is inevitable. Someday, everyone will have to face this reality, and there is no way around it. The only thing we can do is live each day as though it will be the last and pray that when it's our time, we would have fulfilled a purpose that will transcend generations. After a few years of having to go back home for funeral services for family members, I developed a little PTSD (Post-traumatic stress disorder). Anytime I get a call from my family at an unusual time, I would immediately panic and think about what could be wrong. Within the last decade, death started to become a reoccurring reality amongst the people who were a part of the "village" who helped raise me. This wasn't something people around me were dealing with, so I didn't know how to communicate it. There were people around me who hadn't even been to a funeral. This all, of course, turned into me having very morbid thoughts quite often and feeling like this was going to happen year after year, and I would eventually die alone. I started thinking about everyone's death before it would happen, and that was not healthy for me. I started feeling guilty for being away from home before those moments.

I became guilty for not giving my best to my family members before they passed on. I wish I had the chance to express more love and gratitude to ensure they knew how much they meant to me. But what I am working on now to move on from this self-imposed guilt to focus on the memories and the light these people had brought into my life. I realized that the guilt was clouding those good thoughts, and that's what I should focus on because that's what they would want. And anytime I start to have those feelings, I remember to remind myself that their transition wasn't about me.

Ultimately, those were my fears which projected out as anxiety. Some people wish to tie the knot just to identify with those who are married, but again it all became morbid for me. Somehow, I was trying to prevent my biggest fears from happening. The thought of waking up one day to realize that I'm alone hit me like a time bomb. It didn't help at all that I would have nightmares about this, which increased my anxiety every day.

I can recall four or five years ago, how I woke from my sleep crying hysterically, and called my mother on the phone saying, "Mama, please don't leave me, I don't want to be here alone". I can't recall the details of the nightmare, but I believe I started to be more paranoid about death. All this just played out in my thought process because I didn't think anyone would understand me. And I have to be honest, these thoughts still consume me, but I'm learning to grasp hold of them.

I know how challenging it may seem when you have no one around who relates to your circumstances. Or perhaps there could be times you don't want to trouble anyone with what could be seen as trivial or crazy, and then you bottle it up and pretend like everything is ok. That's the unhealthiest thing one can do.

Much later, I found myself where I felt that I had to invalidate my struggles because I knew there were people dealing with struggles far greater than mine. This made me slip into a state where I became unresponsive to my emotions.

I can recall having a complete meltdown, during

a phone conference with my travel business mentor. I remember sitting in my living room in the dark, speaking with her and literally crying the entire call, balling my eyes out. At the other end of the call, she had no clue what was going on because I kept the tears from affecting the tone of my voice. As the call went on, I would keep the phone on mute and would muster up the courage to respond when I could.

Now just to paint the picture more, my mentor gave me ideas and direction for my business, all the resources and tools I could use to grow my business and any other ventures I wanted to partake in. Now why in the world would I have a meltdown at this moment of receiving transformative and cutting edge information that would set me apart. Well, this was happening because I had been dealing with depression and anxiety for some time, and it started to become more frequent. I sat on that call, and my mind went into a complete overdrive that eventually took me off into the deep. I can recall feeling completely overwhelmed, frustrated, lost and hopeless.

My mentor had some great ideas that I wanted to implement, but I was already feeling defeated and unfulfilled. Because I didn't know how I was going to do it all. This led me to feel like I was going to disappoint her or even waste her time. Out of the way, I had flashbacks of my past trauma. All those thoughts combined with those memories coupled with the immediate follow-up of self-loathing. Feeling that I wasn't good enough/ not enough, I could never accomplish major success, you're not worthy of real love, and it's all your fault! For a moment, imagine being on a two-hour conference call, and these are the barrages of thoughts flooding your mind. And it was that night, I first picked up that prescription bottle and just wanted to end it all. I got tired of the voices in my head, even if it was my own voice. I cried all night uncontrollably, my anxiety had completely taken over me, and I didn't know how to unleash the power to control it. I was trying to live up to these high standards that I really knew I wasn't living up to, but I wanted it to seem as if I was. But I was honestly feeling trapped, with no way out.

CHAPTER 4
YOU RELINQUISHED YOUR POWER, NOW WHAT?

"Inner peace begins the moment you choose not to allow another person or event to control your emotions."
—**Pema Chodron**

Have you ever wondered why humans seek to please people or even value their opinion? That was exactly where I found myself, controlled by the opinions and thoughts of others, eventually making me lose focus on God's plans for me.

One of the things I learned most about myself is that I had become a woman who settled for living a life where I was committed to people-pleasing, validation and perfectionism. So much so that I believed I became addicted to it. I thought that this was how I was supposed to operate. I thought that caring what everyone else thought or approved of was how life was designed. For example, when it comes to my parents, hearing their "good job" or "I'm so proud of you, babygirl" became something I chased. As a child, I thought that's what I want to go after. And as I got older, I believe I operated in a state where they could only know the good of me, hiding my poor choices or the consequences of my choices from them to not lose their validation. Now, don't get me wrong, parents being proud of you, celebrating and affirming you is not bad at all. It's a good thing. However, it becomes dangerous to the point when you feed on it and chase it. And I can be honest and say that's what I did. Therapy forced me to learn more about why I did this. Why are you always looking for validation from others, especially your parents? Did your parents say that this was how you're supposed to be? What triggered that cause exactly to the point you begin to relinquish your power to everyone else? No, my parents didn't say that I had to live this way. Of course, they set standards and expectations, which most parents do.

However, as I get older and as I've gone through my journey with mental health, I realized that I had just simply assumed that I had to be perfect for them, whereas they assumed I knew that they knew I was human and bound to make mistakes. What I also realized through therapy and the course of renewing my mind was that although parents no longer have to physically parent their child(ren) once they become adults, they continue to learn and grow along with them into adulthood, still learning and adjusting their mindset. Once I started to become more vulnerable with my parents, I felt this immediate release and pressure to not always have to get it right. DO I still sometimes believe that I have to? Yes, but now I can recognize it, adjust and move beyond it.

Another area that me relinquishing my power was dominant, as you could imagine, was definitely my dating life. Whew! In so many ways, I allowed how men viewed me to validate my worthiness of being loved. Just like most people, my heart has been broken a few times. But that's part of life, right? It's inevitable. However, I'm learning more that heartbreak doesn't equal unworthiness. I think I missed out on that clarification somewhere. Once I fell in love, I believed that person's approval became a piece of the image I saw of myself. Once there was a "disapproval" or "invalidation" of me or parts of me, I always seem to let it chip off a layer of my self-confidence. And after so long, I left myself with the bare minimum. Only loving those parts that were consistently validated.

If you are a fan of the Starz hit TV show titled "Power[3]" you'd be familiar with Ghost the main character, who seems to have it all together with the outside world: money, family, career, living the dream life. However, unknown to people who were alien to his inner circle, he was living a double life.

During the show, Ghost consistently tried to run away from the life he no longer felt served him. He let go of it but was constantly sucked back in.

As I take inventory of Ghost's lifestyle, I look past the drugs, money, fast life, and everything else that it entails. I could see that the story is an outline of the battle that many of us deal with somehow. In Ghost's life, I see a man who lived in the world he created for himself and wanted to change it. It was difficult to let go of who he no longer wanted to be and also please everyone else. Perhaps, some lovers of this TV show may disagree with this fact and instead argue that Ghost did everything to benefit himself. To an extent that is true, however, I believe he was trying to also fit into the mold of people around him while trying to maintain who he wanted to be. Eventually, both identities became a challenge.

Now, I realize that I've been trying to live up to the

---

3 https://www.tvguide.com/tvshows/power/cast/617435/

standard of people and the pressures that society has placed on women. For am I now trying to win the favor of people or God? Or am I striving to please people? If I were still trying to please people, I would not be a slave of Christ." Galatians 1:10 I was always careful not to disappoint anyone (well try to at least), and at the same time, I wanted to be true myself. You see, it is difficult to keep a dual identity.

For this reason, I have written this book as an anthology of self-healing, therapeutic dose and personal restoration from the grip of depression, anxiety, trauma bondage and limiting beliefs. I agree with Maya Angelou, who once said, "there is no greater agony than bearing an untold story inside you." I believe in the inherent power of writing, and this is the first time I'll share personal matters of my life without paying any attention to whatever people think.

Through therapy, I discovered that I had unknowingly relinquished the power God placed on the inside of me to everyone else but myself for most of my life. And that set a standard for what I allowed in my life. When you aren't truly happy with yourself from the inside out, you look for other things or people to make you happy.

At the same time, my career was no longer fulfilling me. My travel business quietly started to feel like a burden, and I had little to no drive to continue operating it. I looked for my most important relationships to bring the happiness and savor I craved for, but only the bad parts started to be the focal point, becoming overwhelming. Therapy allowed me to embrace self-love. Over the years, I allowed situations and certain people to define how I loved and viewed myself and that, of course, was an unhealthy thing to do. I also allowed the labels that have been placed on me since being a child to define my actions and self-worth as an adult. Therapy uncovered that I was still holding on to "little girl Kelsey". This is what most therapists define as holding on to your inner child and that it's imperative to heal your inner child. "Little girl Kelsey" had in some ways not grown-up or let go of those insecurities that formed during that time. I would dim my light to run away from the labels people placed on me or just how they made me feel about myself. And quite naturally, I brought all those insecurities into adulthood, often becoming defensive.

Instead of allowing God and myself to define who I was, I allowed everyone else to do it, which made me live my life trying not to disappoint anyone even those who didn't truly care about me.

When you get so preoccupied to please people or

prevent them from rejecting you, you end up letting yourself down. I made everyone's opinion my reality, and that neither brought honor to God nor was it fair to me. We can empower people to take on the driver's seat of our life without knowing it.

RELATIONSHIPS VERSUS ME

One of the healthiest relationships you'll ever have is a relationship with yourself. Because that is the starting point to true happiness and fulfillment in life.

One of the hardest revelations I had to come to terms with was the attitude I portrayed within my relationships while dealing with frustrations and internal battles. This is not limited to my romantic relationship but also relationships with loved ones. It took me a while to understand that I was projecting my internal frustrations externally, and a few of those that I loved were caught in the crossfire. This was the hardest thing to admit, but it was my reality.

At some point, I wasn't myself, and I struggled to get back to myself. As I described in chapter three- Mind Playing Tricks, my thoughts literally consumed me daily, especially at night.

To be honest, relationships are a driving force in life. Life revolves around it, from your relationship with God, your relationship with yourself, family, friends, work and love. They all hold integral parts that determine the course of our lives. When healing is required, more than likely, fears and insecurities exist, which heightens depression and anxiety. And when those insecurities and fears aren't dealt with properly, they are projected onto others.

For years, I gradually became more and more frustrated with certain people in my life, and sadly, I had to hold up the perfection side of the relationships I had. I became aggrieved with the onus to be the people-pleaser, thereby making the other party happy, irrespective of how I felt. In turn, hurt people hurt people.

In some of those relationships, I would voice the "double standards" that were consistently displayed. Sadly, each time I brought it up, it usually seemed to fall on deaf ears. In all conscience, I typically get infuriated, yet I wouldn't communicate. In truth, I felt unappreciated and taken for granted in these relationships. However, I learned a lesson. I realized that irrespective of how much you sacrifice for someone, they may not reciprocate it. So, I shouldn't keep my hopes high. There's a saying that "one good turn deserves another." Of course; why not! As true as it may sound, it's possible to do for others, hope for the best possible return, yet get betrayed and disappointed. As humans, we have the notion that everyone should think and act like we do, especially when we feel that we are giving wholeheartedly in various ways. Regrettably, sometimes we get disappointed.

Although I became so frustrated with those one-sided relationships, I had to admit that I created these relationships myself in some ways. I had set the standard for how I allowed others to treat me. And, maybe because I'd allowed them to treat me the way they did, they may have felt like, "well, this is how it's always been," and probably thought, "Why are you upset about it now?" And then some may not have even recognized what they were doing if I never truly corrected the situation.

I told myself that I owed myself the responsibility to be happy. And when you truly love yourself, love from other people is like a bonus. Therapy has taught me that it's not about anyone else; it's about me. When I first started with my current therapist, I talked more about how other people felt, how I don't want anyone else in a bad space, yet I couldn't seem to care or fully focus on myself. It was time to stop putting my relationship with others before the relationship I had with myself. I was pouring into these relationships, yet I was losing out on me.

I realize that me not ending relationships or friendships wasn't about me loving hard. Yes, I have a big heart but that doesn't justify me accepting people in my life who took advantage of me and who didn't respect boundaries. Yet, it was simply me being afraid to lose someone, thinking that would then define me. I allowed certain people to provide the bare minimum in order to be a part of my life. And allowing them to do so produces relationships of bondage and not joy.

A BATTLE FOR ACCEPTANCE

I started subscribing to the notion that acceptance was the goal. That how others viewed your circumstances was what we used to justify standard and approval. We are all familiar with the negative connotation of the labels of "silver spoon" and "spoiled". Well, those labels followed me for the majority of my life. Over time, it was something I tried to run away from. Those labels led me to develop this extreme independence, especially with my parents, even when I really needed their help. My older sister and I dealt with this our entire childhoods.

We would get either penalized, rejected or criticized for being in a two-parent middle-class household. My parents worked very hard to provide a better life for their children. I am thankful to God that I can say I don't remember ever going without anything. However, that doesn't mean my parents didn't see any hard times. They just made sure we didn't see it.

My sister and I would catch it from everyone, from the church folks, extended family members to friends. Often hearing "she got a mama and daddy" or "you always get what you want, don't you". I'm not going to lie and say I never asked my parents for anything, what child doesn't? And I can recall my mother's response anytime I mentioned what someone said, "You're my child, don't worry about what anyone says". She never wanted us to feel bad for having two parents who loved us and wanted to provide. But, I didn't listen to her. I allowed others' opinions about me being brought up in a two-parent household get to me, becoming hesitant even stating that that was my family dynamic.

I continued to hear it through the years, and over time, learned to ignore it. But, those comments turned my sense of independence to this point where I felt like I had to prove to everyone that I didn't need my parents. There were many times I went without because I just didn't want to ask my parents because I would hear those comments in my head. Times where when they had to, it gave me complete anxiety. However, one of the last times was within my first year of entering corporate America, and a "friend" felt a way that my parents were still helping me financially. I was immediately upset, trying to figure out why that was even a discussion as it wasn't something I discussed with them directly. Again, I was confused but at this point annoyed. And I let it be known that I was bothered by that. I shouldn't have to explain why my parents were helping their child who had been unemployed for two years while in graduate school get on her feet and adjust. I eventually had to start checking myself on this, giving people that much authority to get me upset and feel guilty for what God blessed me with.

Ultimately, I realized those people weren't mad at me. They were frustrated with their own circumstances. I learned two lessons here, don't take the fall for others' circumstances and keep your business to yourself. It wasn't something I went around boasting about, but when you meet people, and they get to know you, they eventually find out that your parents are married and raised you together. It did confuse me, but I got so tired of hearing it that I would avoid talking about my parents in certain cases. Which, of course, was difficult because my parents play huge roles in my life. It got to the point of not talking about my upbringing, it created a sense of independence within me.. At first, it was to prove I wasn't spoilt and my parents weren't providing everything for me. It molded my personality to become determined and ambitious, with the desire to go any length to do anything for my parents, no matter how big or small it was. So I allowed the effects of others' circumstances to influence me to downplay my blessings that I am so grateful for.

NOW WHAT?

We don't always just give power to other people but to things, situations or events. I gave so much power to my past. Consistently living there, talking about it, and so concentrated on not allowing the past to happen again. Why are we so reluctant to let go of the past and not allow it to have power over us? I believe it's because we know what the past looks like. There are no questions about the past, because it already happened. There are no unknowns in the past. I constantly used the past as a guide to how the future would be. For instance, if I couldn't achieve a goal in the past,

I convinced myself I wouldn't try again. Don't get me wrong; I know that letting go of the past is not an easy feat. It's the hardest thing one could ever do.

The power we give to our past allows it to live in our minds rent-free for longer than it should be. And constantly living in the past creates a negative spirit can also be a grieving spirit when sadness is attached. Journaling has become more of an outlet for me than anything since starting therapy. My therapist ensures that before ending my sessions that I have a homework exercise. And sometimes, these exercises involve writing. Those assignments would lead me to simply write my thoughts down to release and understand what's going with me. This would also make it easier for me to present my thoughts and feelings in therapy. When I discovered how much power I had given others, of course, prompted me to figure out ways to release that power and no longer be bound to that limiting belief.

So instead of finding comfort in giving my power away, I found my power in the word STOP. Now, this doesn't mean that I took my power back overnight, but I created a method, a reminder to recognize how not to relinquish my power. What if there was some alarm that went off anytime you relinquished your power to someone else other than yourself or God? If such an alarm existed, I'm sure there would be a lot of unhappy people (takers), and you would be walking and living in favor of God.

THE POWER OF STOP

1. Stop giving your Power to Anyone Else...especially to make you or to make your life different.
2. Stop allowing the disappointments of others to define who you are and your worth.
3. Stop looking for repayment for anything you've done for anyone else.
4. Stop allowing the potential of who someone could be to distract you from who they really are.
5. Stop assuming that your perspective on things is the same perceptive others have.
6. Stop allowing unfulfilled (not YET obtained) chapters of your life to determine the trajectory of your life.
7. Stop allowing other people's schedules to become your schedule.
8. Stop living in the past of pain and hurt; it no longer serves you.

PART 2:
THE DISCOVERY

CHAPTER 5
MOVING BEYOND IT ALL

"Although the world is full of suffering, it is also full of the overcoming of it."

—Helen Keller

What if there was a place we could all go with all our problems, thoughts and feelings and exchange them for everything we want? I'm not going to pretend I wouldn't check it out to see if it's legit and, if so, see how many exchanges I could make in one year. The reality is there will never be an actual place for us to make such exchanges, but we do have resources and tools to assist us with managing our problems, thoughts and feelings. My focus is on building a strong foundation within myself that depicts healing and peace.

Therapy is now that safe space for me to release pain, understand my thoughts and emotions, discuss my "why's", and let go of anything that's burdening me. Therapy is not a quick fix! You must do the WORK and it will take time and commitment. Be patient.

Moving beyond depression and anxiety comes with equipping yourself with knowledge and allowing some guidance to be an addition. It would have taken me a very long time to move beyond depression (anxiety is something I still have to monitor) without really tapping into it to understand it better and know how to navigate my way out of it.

UNDERSTANDING DEPRESSION & ANXIETY

The key to understanding depression and anxiety is knowing the signs and symptoms. One major benefit of my journey is the education I've received along the way. Whether from my therapist, at the hospital—, or the findings I made from my research, they went a long way to make me better. Before I visited the hospital, I didn't know how to define my mood changes. I knew that I would have my low moments that would last maybe a few hours to a day. Or I would have extreme low moments that could last for multiple days.

I knew I was becoming more out-of-focus and,

eventually, losing myself. I can recall stating out loud, "I'm depressed," but I don't believe I truly understood what being depressed meant. But I know that I had mood swings, and sometimes, they lasted for a long while, which concerned me. These occurrences are what most medical practitioners would categorize as a depressive episode. Today's medical news defines a depressive episode in the context of a major depressive disorder as a period characterized by low moods and other depression symptoms that lasts two weeks or more. Depression and anxiety may not be the same for everyone. So it's important to recognize some of the key signs if you are struggling with it or suspect that someone you know is going through it. I highly suggest asking for professional help even if that's simply a consultation that includes describing how you feel and then going from there.

It is important to note that depression or anxiety should not be overlooked or ignored! Do you know why? It can aggravate and result in a more complex situation. You may have come across someone who probably doesn't believe that depression is real, or you may be that person. The truth is, there's nothing wrong with that. Most people believe depression is just a thing of the mind and may probably not demand so much from the physical body. Well, that's true.

Depression does impact the brain! However, it definitely can impact the physical body. Our physical and mental makeup is so complex, and when there is a problem, both the body and mind will respond.[4]

Here are some of the signs of depression you can look out for:

- Persistent Sadness
- Loss of Interest
- Lack of Focus
- Decreased Energy
- Insomnia
- Appetite and Weight Changes
- Thoughts of Death or Suicide
- Restlessness or Irritability
- Aches or pains with no physical causes[5]

Here are some of the signs of anxiety you must look out for:

- Excessive Worry
- Feeling Agitated
- Restlessness

---

4 Health.havard.edu/topics/depression
5 Heathline.com/health/depression

- Fatigue
- Difficulty Concentrating
- Irritability
- Tense Muscles
- Panic Attacks
- Avoiding Social Situations
- Irrational Fears[6]

Before I went to the hospital, I had already taken the first step and began therapy. Honestly, it took me over a year to make the first step and commit to going. Many factors were stopping me, mostly just feeling like I didn't need it. I usually feel I'll just be fine. Telling myself, "You're ok and do not have any behavior problems." This was the sad reality of my viewpoints of what mental illness looked like. So, I thought I could handle this just the same. I didn't realize that my problems had aggravated more than I imagined.

I'm a huge fan of the 90s era, from the music (specifically R&B) to the classic tv shows. One of my favorite hit sitcoms is Living Single. It's about four African-American women who are all in their careers and stages of love and romance.

---

6 Https://www.healthline.com/health/anxiety-symptoms

In writing this book, I was randomly watching the episode[7] where the lead character, Khadijah James, played by the legendary Queen Latifah, was under enormous amounts of stress with running her magazine company and managing her life outside of it. When she decided to see a therapist, she kept it a secret and even felt the need to disguise herself. In watching this episode, it stood out differently. Indeed, we've come a long way with mental health since the 90s. Yet, there are still those same stigmas to overcome. In the session, the therapist told her that she could be dealing with either anxiety or depression based on the information Khadijah provided. Khadijah's reaction was like one who was in denial concerning the ailment, with tainted ideations of those who are indeed depressed—like people who sit around, eating cookie dough all day, and cry at random commercials.

The therapist had to correct her by giving her insight and clarity about what depression really is and what triggers it. Then, she discovered that Khadijah was dealing with much deeper emotional constraints and needed to take some time off and come visit her again. As a matter of fact, most good sitcoms tackle real-life issues, even with some comic relief,

---

7 https://www.tvguide.com/tvshows/living-single/episodes-sea-son-3/1000131819/

to be able to bring more awareness. This episode only gave me even more confirmation that I am doing the right things to take better care of myself, and it's nothing to be ashamed of.

Let me be the first to say that finding a therapist is a process, especially when you don't know what to look for. All I knew is that I wanted a woman of color and for my insurance to be accepted. So, I searched till I found one who fulfilled those two qualifications. However, I still had to come out of pocket because my insurance didn't fully cover the expense. I had my first session, and I remember walking in and sitting on a couch just like I envisioned from having watched tv.

When I got in, I sat there and spilled my guts for about 20 minutes. I can remember how she looked at me and said, "you're very self-aware." This didn't come to me as a shock because I knew what most of my issues were on the surface. I felt accomplished at the end of the session, although I felt I didn't need therapy based on the feedback I received. But I had made myself a promise to do this and see it through.

The plan was to do these sessions once a month and then see how I felt later on to do more. I continued with the sessions and eventually started them via telephone. And honestly, it was the same as being physically present. I spilled my guts and got some feedback; yet, deep down, I didn't feel like it was worth the extra bill every month. However, I refused to admit it. Then, I had one more session with that therapist. And, honestly, it was pretty much the same again. In an actual sense, I didn't know if this was normal. I felt like I just needed to give it more time.

However, it became a little difficult to schedule more sessions, which pushed me to find other options. So, I began my search again, still wanting to find a woman of color and have my insurance accepted. But also who seemed more relatable and gave more in-depth feedback and something to think about after each session. This time, I was going to take a different approach because I knew just what I needed, so I was going to take my time in my search. I realized that those who offered free consultations helped me vett out and see who would be a good fit.

Understand that I am not saying my first therapist was not good; she just wasn't a good fit for me. In seeking a therapist, you must be sure you get the one who will be able to offer the help you need. Emphasis on YOU! Thus, you must take it seriously, not assume that all therapists are the same and not stop searching for the right person. It's the same as finding a doctor, dentist, lawyer, hair stylist, personal trainer, and more. The truth is, everyone is simply not meant for everyone, and that is perfectly okay. I am sharing this part of my journey for anyone who may have started therapy and, because of a similar experience, have given up or are considering it. Hold on, Sis! Don't give up! Instead, try again.

After researching for about a week, I had narrowed down to three therapists that I wanted to speak with. Surprisingly, I didn't make it past the first consultation because it was a perfect fit for me, especially because she is still my therapist. My sessions were set for two times per month via video conference. My sessions were more vulnerable, where I showed my emotions and opened up even more. It only took one session for me to recognize the difference and that it was exactly what I needed.

SEEK AND YOU SHALL FIND

Finding the right therapist for you (keywords, right and you) should not be an overwhelming undertaking, but it can be if you don't know what to look for. Like I mentioned early on, my current therapist is not my first therapist, and that's okay. If you have not started therapy and are looking to obtain one, be patient and trust the process. However, it doesn't have to take an extremely long time to find the right want to do this in a judge-free zone, free from negative body language or disciplinary tones.

5. At the end of that first conversation, did you leave with something? In my opinion, it's important that every session, you walk away with something, whether that's clarity, a breakthrough or a sense of relief from something.

BREAKING THE CYCLE

I think about how easy it has always been for me to encourage and support other people, but it was so difficult to encourage myself. And I don't want to be someone who doesn't live up to the things they post or say when trying to spread positivity for others. We all know the definition of insanity, doing the same thing over and over and getting the same result. And that's what I realized I was doing with my life. Don't get me wrong, yes, I'm blessed and have accomplished so much, but I know if I continue with the same mindset, harboring unforgiveness and self-loathing, I wouldn't get the very best of life that God has for me.

Honestly, I didn't ever see myself going for therapy because I believed in the stigmas surrounding it. The thought fit. In some ways, I feel lucky that it didn't take me but two tries because I have heard others have different experiences. For that reason, I want to share this checklist with you to better you on your journey in finding the right therapist.

Here are my personal questions that you can ask yourself when finding the right therapist for you:

1. Who do you want to sit across from as you describe and detail what you're going through and need help in figuring out? It's your personal preference. Note that this is not solely just in regards to race, but also gender and age range.

2. Are you confident in their abilities and background to treat you? Research your potential therapist, review their education and also their areas of focus. Oh, and checking their reviews doesn't hurt either.

3. How will I be able to pay for therapy? Review your current expenses, look at your health insurance (or speak with your provider to understand your mental health coverage) and budget out what you can afford.

4. Did the therapist provide a safe, comfortable space? When it comes to vulnerability, most people

of sitting down with a stranger to share my business did not appeal to me. But now, I realize that was immature thinking, and I was ignorant to what therapy is, who it is for and its benefits.

Often, we depend on family and friends for our only counsel. Trust me, there is nothing wrong with confiding in a loved one. However, it's also better to get opinions, insight and direction from someone who does not have an emotional tie to you. That's what gave me more comfort in therapy. I'd sit there, speaking with someone who doesn't have any stake in my life that can be truthful, raw, and uncut. I am truly grateful for my support system. I know that I am blessed to be surrounded by people who genuinely love me and want the best for me. But there were times where I felt judged and misunderstood. Even times where I felt like I was being reprimanded for feeling the way that I felt and being told to simply shake things off. So, naturally, I would shut down and try to process and deal with everything on my own. The reality of it is that depressed people are generally put into the category of negativity and toxicity, making it difficult for others to understand and/or being around them.

Let me tell you what I love about therapy, it calls me out from an in-depth place that no one has ever taken me before. One of the things my therapist recognized and called me out about was that I tried to pull myself out of depression as if I wasn't depressed, as if I had no issues and nothing to heal from. Instead, she wanted me to understand that it was okay to feel vulnerable and feel low at times. The key is to be in those feelings, recognize and understand them and then work my way beyond them. Also, she let it be known you have to be open and ready to discover the real deep rooted issues and problems, and where they come from. Another thing my therapist has to do repeatedly is remind me of where a "Why" of mine stems from when it comes to me always taking blame and feeling responsible for everyone's feelings and actions. And I promise every time, it's like hearing it the first time. I'll tell her about a situation, how I reacted and how I felt about something, and she would always direct me back to the root. And it'll all make sense because this has been my norm for me for so long. For a moment, I would be upset with myself for forgetting that but she always reminds me that I've been living this way for so long that it's going to take time to readjust and remember my why. And pulling me back before heading towards a dangerous downward spiral of would of, should of, could of! I stopped solely coping with the triggers of my depression instead I learned how to heal from the underlying causes.

If I can go back in time to the very point I began to mentally and emotionally struggle, I would tell myself to stop looking for people, things or even just time to heal my pain and that the only person that can heal me is me. And that includes the work I put into myself. Also, recognizing that holding on to it all can affect me physically. I can recall one time in the thick of a depressive episode, literally fighting to get out of bed to get to the store and also just trying to get out of the house, thinking I would feel better. It was as if I was physically sick. I gradually managed to shower and get dressed, but my body and mind were simply not cooperating. After about 3 attempts, I managed to get in the car and drive to the store. I remember walking around and somewhat holding my breath, fighting to keep it together physically. In my mind, if I exhaled, I would immediately break down right then and there. I was filled with so much anxiety but knew I needed to get out. As soon as I opened the door to my home, I fell to my knees. I exhaled and felt relieved that I had made it. I managed to keep it together long enough until I no longer had to physically carry the weight of that episode.

And now, therapy has become the foundation of healing for me. I've discovered that most of us don't always have the tools and resources to know what to do when life happens and how to recover from any of it. Most of us usually wallow in the sea of confusion, so it seems hard to recover from the impact, especially because we don't understand our mind's emotional state. Therapy is indeed a tool one uses to sort out, face and discover the core of what's going on inside and so much more. So, it's time to break the cycle of brushing things under the rug and masking the pain.

Therapy has completely changed my life. It doesn't mean that I'm perfect, nor do I have it all figured out. But therapy is a space for me to unpack my thoughts of past and current events. Through therapy, I have discovered new, effective ways to show up in my life.

If you're not mentally ready for the next level in your life, you can't get there.

THERAPY PLUS PEACE

In the long run, my journey to seek a therapeutic dose brought peace. Peace will bring stability and position you for victory, give you a sense of inner harmony and mental sync, which are an important baseline for happiness and productivity.

In my opinion, there is no better feeling than having peace of mind. It will generate every other positive feeling and emotion. Additionally, when you have peace, you can find joy in times of sorrow, you can find happiness after a dark moment, and you can be content with your purpose and personality.

However, I've realized that peace doesn't mean everything is perfect; it means having the ability to walk on top of the storms of life unperturbed. It means having the courage to walk away from anyone or anything that seeks to sap your peace.

END OF THE TUNNEL

It might sound cliché, but there is light at the end of every tunnel. The strength of overcoming is what defines you, not the pain. If you are someone who is going through my "chapter 1", just know that you can push through that chapter and find yourself in the next chapter, then the next and so forth. Allow yourself to feel the pain. It's a vital and powerful aspect of your healing process.

Therapy has taught me how to be more vulnerable, and that vulnerability is molding me into a new person that understands the why's of things instead. I'm using what I've heard Charlamagne tha God often speaks about, divine misdirection, to adjust my perception on the trajectory of my life. A lot of the things that felt like disappointments and failures turned out to be the best things for me or great lessons as I transition into this new phase, develop and mature. Growing into a woman and moving from the "woman girl" phase. The phase where you're physically a woman but in many ways are still holding onto the little girl inside. How I viewed people either voluntarily or involuntarily leaving my life as heartaches or a no to a job offer I wanted, it was simply God looking out. When your life increases and expands without them, you realize that it was necessary for your journey.

CHAPTER 6
DON'T MINIMIZE YOUR BREAKTHROUGH

"God is our source of strength. Lean on him. Trust in the Lord with all your heart and lean not on your own understanding."

—Proverbs 3:5

My hope with this book is that you are moved to action to break against your barriers, and the stigmas society holds in order to unpack, confront and correct. Let me make one thing perfectly clear, therapy is NOT a substitution for prayer and having a relationship with God. Before finding solace in therapy, I honestly wasn't fully seeking God as I should have. It got to a point where I thought either God had left me or was punishing me. The little girl who grew up in the church, who would go for service weekly, who most times understood the lessons and sermons, grew into an adult that found herself questioning God's love for her.

Those thoughts didn't make me stay away from church but as I reflect now, I know that I was just going through the motions. All I knew was that Sundays were for church, and that's where I was supposed to be even when I was struggling. I recognized that I wasn't feeding and cultivating my faith enough. Hey! Don't get me wrong! That doesn't imply I lost my faith in that God is indeed real. I wasn't nurturing my relationship with Him to where I wouldn't question His love for me. Although I didn't verbalize it—but one day, I found out I didn't know how to approach God anymore. At some point, I was too ashamed to go to God. I was so lost I just ended up suppressing it. And that suppression, amongst others, only elevated my depression and anxiety.

Yes, I would call His name out in my darkest moments, but I wasn't seeking Him as I should have been. And it wasn't until after I got truly vulnerable in therapy and started to understand what therapy was and why I needed it that I began to recognize that spiritual life is connected to mental life. The mind, body and spirit are interconnected, and when one is off, others will be impacted.

PAIN IS TEMPORARY

Therapy helped me to understand that pain is temporary. Just like the former American professional cyclist puts it, Lance Armstrong once said, "Pain is temporary. It may last a minute, or an hour, or a day, or a year, but eventually it will subside..." You see, this universal truth holds for every situation. Therapy helped me to understand that pain is indeed temporary. As I go through therapy, read, meditate and find gratitude in my journey, I've come to understand that the core of strength is pain. We often find ourselves in a space where we believe that we are strong because we don't break down when life gets hard, however, our strength is greater when we break down but then break through.

God didn't say we wouldn't go through pain or heartache; however, He promised that we would get through it.

Paul learned to classify his pain and suffering as "light affliction, which is but for a moment is working for us a far more exceeding and eternal weight of glory..." 2 Corinthians 4:17. Could you be on the verge of victory despite walking through the valley of broken vines? Have you ever gone through a rough time, and then before you know it, you're looking back like, "How did I manage to overcome all of that"?

This is simply because God promises to provide us with resources to get us through the pain. That's why I truly believe that therapy is a gift from God. And consulting self-help experts does not reveal weakness but strength.

My biggest obstacle has been letting go of my pain. It appeared that as much as I wanted it to be released, I wanted to hold onto it just as much, if not more. Subconsciously, me holding on to it allowed me to maintain my walls of defensiveness or perhaps prevent me from going through any other trauma ever again. I thought if I held on to those things that hurt me, I could prevent them from happening again. That mindset only kept me in the dark, a place of pain, and a place of feeling trapped. I didn't know that I needed to heal. I just thought that all I had to do was move on with life. But now I understand that you truly can't move on in life if you are holding on to it, and the only way to let go of that pain is to let yourself heal.

As you are aware, pain is unpleasant and intolerable, and the natural human response is to exchange pain for relief wherever it may be found.

When we experience pain at various points in time, we want to exchange it for something that feels better. For instance, any sick person naturally wants to get well; people who are enduring grief from losing a loved one would do anything to have them back. Likewise, everyone going through mental or psychological trauma desperately craves relief.

THERAPY PLUS GOD (SPIRITUAL GROWTH)

Therapy made me realize that I'd stopped putting my trust in God. Although I believed that He is real and powerful, I wasn't putting Him at the center of my life. I wanted to be in control, and I wanted to ensure certain things happened to me and for me. I got back to the core of honoring that God wants the best for me, and He has the final say in my life. He has provided us with remedies for every situation.

I now truly believe that God meant for us to have this resource as He meant for us to have doctors, lawyers, dentists, etc. Man alone cannot do it all. But while we are praising God, asking Him for forgiveness, asking Him to order our steps, asking for discernment and understanding, we can lean on earthly resources such as therapy to help break down what we are going to the Most High for.

In the Living Single episode[8], I mentioned in Chapter 5, when Khadijah first said that she didn't need a therapist; all she needed was to go to church, "get herself some Jesus." Her therapist affirmed that it's a popular choice yet presented the view that "God must have created therapists for a reason." The reality of it is, we're taught to give our all to God. But, the question is, what if we don't know what to give over to him or pray about? We may know the situation, but we're just praying for the situation and missing out on a breakthrough point. For me, that is what therapy is, clarity! When you are clear on what you want, you'll be more specific with what you request, and your bond with God will become even stronger.

Therapy has allowed me to get to the root of many things and have the ability to know what I can change and what I can't. We can all benefit from alone time with God because we get so lost and busy in our lives that we don't hear the heart of him and the directions he is trying to provide for the course of our journeys. My therapy sessions aren't religious or spiritual driven, they're based on cognitive correlation to my life. However,

---

8 https://www.tvguide.com/tvshows/living-single/episodes-season-3/1000131819/

that doesn't mean that my therapist doesn't believe in God or wants to lead me away from my own spiritual beliefs. When it comes to therapy, research shows that many therapists are hesitant to include religion or spirituality, due to differences that could potentially spark controversy, defeating the sole purpose for someone seeking therapy. So, if you are someone who wants to have a more spiritual-based treatment, then consider seeking out a spiritual advisor. To be honest, I don't think there would be anything wrong with having both a clinical therapist and a spiritual counselor, especially if you're looking to strengthen your spirituality and mental health at the same time. This is you utilizing available resources to learn how to meditate on God's word to strengthen the key areas of your life.

THERAPY PLUS FORGIVENESS

Over time, the choices we make create the world we live in. This could be simultaneously liberating and sobering. It means that you cannot totally blame people for where you are. One part of therapy you must understand is the power of forgiveness. Don't you wonder why forgiving someone can be the hardest thing to do? Why do we need to forgive at all?

Why is there a process when it comes to forgiveness?

A renowned Christian author and professor of theology, Louis B. Smedes, once said, To forgive is to set a prisoner free and discover that the prisoner was you[9]." This means that forgiveness has impacted your mental and physical well-being. Out rightly, speaking forgiveness is for yourself and not the other person. Ultimately, you give yourself not only to change the narrative but also to obtain a new life script. However, what if the person you're upset with is you. Self-forgiveness can be the hardest kind of forgiveness.

Apologize and Forgive Yourself- Give Yourself Some Grace... God Does.

Do you often refuse to forgive yourself because you think God has not or won't forgive you for choices you made in your mind? I, for a long time, could not utter the words let alone actually take action to forgive myself for being in a situation with a man that would take advantage of me. I remember being extremely disappointed that I would put myself down more than I ever did before. Everything that has ever happened to me, I would somehow redirect the outcome

9 https://www.brainyquote.com/quotes/lewis_b_smedes_135524

back to me. I've always believed in taking accountability for my actions no matter what. I was a critical analytic, and I

would analyze a situation repeatedly and end up right back at me as the problem. But who am I to not forgive myself when God forgives me daily? I recall the words from Lamentations 3:21;23, which says, "The steadfast love of the LORD never ceases; his mercies never come to an end; 23they are new every morning; great is your faithfulness."

CHAPTER 7
DEVELOPING VERBAL HABITS

"Your beliefs become your thoughts, Your thoughts become your words."

—Gandhi

The most important words we will ever hear are the words we say to ourselves. Therapy has taught me so much about myself, about my experiences, and most importantly, how to talk to myself. Yes, that's what I said, how I talk to myself! We grow up thinking that talking to yourself and/or even answering yourself, means you must be CRAZY. Actually, those conversations with yourself are extremely important. Now, I don't mean that when you're out shopping or dining have a full-blown discussion with yourself, this, unfortunately, will alarm someone, and it may get awkward. Therapy teaches me how to have those crucial private conversations with myself. For me, this is the core of the

95

"work" that comes with therapy. As I mentioned, therapy isn't a quick fix or an overnight remedy; it's a journey. So with any journey comes some work, and typically that work is about exploring unfamiliar areas. In this chapter, I will discuss some of the key verbal habits I personally had to either break or make anew.

When you live with someone for an extended period of time, you naturally become accustomed to their habits and to their presence. You adjust your behavior and habits to coexist with theirs in order to provide peace and harmony. Metaphorically speaking, when we adjust to life with our "inner critic," we aren't creating that same peace and harmony. We're actually causing conflict. For a long time, I made room and space for my "inner critic" to dwell in my internal home. I allowed this "inner critic" to say horrible things to me, stop me from stepping out of my comfort zone, and became paranoid of everyone around me, questioning every word said or action taken. Full-on fighting a war in my mind 24/7, 365! Not realizing that holding on to my inner critic will only hinder me from becoming better and finding peace.

Communicate Your Boundaries- Set Them and Don't let up...

Unless You Want To

"No one will listen to us until we listen to ourselves."

—Marianne Williamson

Prior to therapy, I honestly didn't understand how to set boundaries. I really didn't know that's what I should have been learning and doing. Most of the time, when we think of boundaries, we assume it's solely for other people. However, I've learned that those boundaries can be created with ourselves as well. Whether it's how we separate work from our personal lives or even how we set boundaries on how much we indulge in guilty pleasures. Not setting boundaries in life can be a limiting belief. We sometimes, as humans, are so caught up in satisfying our wants and not our needs that we don't place structure to allow for peace to exist. Therapy helped me to recognize that I wouldn't set boundaries for other people nor myself. When dealing with others, I would always feel guilty for even considering setting boundaries. By setting boundaries with people, especially those I loved, I thought that I was being selfish and inconsiderate. I thought that because I love them, setting boundaries would somehow minimize the love I have for them. However, I've realized if anything should strengthen that relationship, which in turn the love grows. Boundaries also help determine whether a relationship is worth having. When you set boundaries, and people don't respect them, you, in turn, have a choice to make, and that's whether to continue allowing that person to be in your life. Yes, I get it. Sometimes cutting people out of your life is not the easiest thing, nor am I saying it's the only option you have. I believe it should be the last result after all options have been explored. Communicating your boundaries is very important in maintaining your mental health. Don't get me wrong, when someone doesn't respect your boundaries, it doesn't necessarily make them a bad person. You would be surprised by how many people don't understand boundaries and how to not cross them. Like I mentioned earlier, respecting boundaries with yourself is just as crucial. One thing is for sure; therapy will help you be accountable for the boundaries you set with you and everyone else.

I no longer see therapy as a selfish act but a wise one. Our prayer to God shouldn't always be about him fixing everything in our lives or giving us everything that we want. We should be going into prayer, asking God to grant us wisdom, knowledge and a sound mind to make good decisions and judgment calls in our lives. Will we always use that wisdom? No! In reality, you can try to be everything to everybody, but that leaves no room for yourself to grow and understand what it is that you need out of life. We hear it often that it's okay to say, "No" sometimes. It's because you need those boundaries. There was a period of time where I put myself in isolation. I wasn't active on social media, I didn't hang out; I simply kept to myself. I needed that time to really focus on my healing. And I can truly say it helped me.

Before you can communicate your boundaries, you must first define what they are and your reasons for setting them. Communicate with yourself and then to others. Here are some steps in creating your boundaries and how to set them:

1. Permit yourself. Release any guilt or doubt regarding the potential responses you may receive. Place your self-respect first and then go forth.

2. Tap into your feelings. Where does your discomfort, frustration and/or instability lie?

3. Check yourself. Let's get real....you may find yourself at some point not sustaining your boundaries, and that's okay. Be self-aware, refocus and then re-enforce.

4. Commit and Assert. When you've established your

boundaries, become one with them and address these boundaries head-on with others, leaving no room for misunderstanding.

5. Have Accountability Partner(s). Support can be a crucial part of maintaining boundaries. Find your circle that understands and respects your boundaries so that they can hold you accountable.

I DARE YOU TO RECOGNIZE YOUR TRIGGERS

"Be Sure You Positively identify your target before you pull the trigger."

—Tom Flynn

Triggers, by far the most revealing aspect of my journey since starting therapy. I realized before, I really didn't understand or even fully know all my triggers. I could recognize them in some cases, but it wouldn't be until after I reacted. See here's the thing....no matter where you are in your mental health journey or even just in life, there will always be some type of trigger, especially if you are working your way to overcome trauma. The goal is to know what they are, understand them, why they are what they are and work on moving past them. However, that doesn't mean you aren't still going to be susceptible to being affected by them. Some triggers may be unavoidable while some triggers can be eradicated altogether.

Therapy will indeed assist you in identifying your triggers. You may discover triggers that you least expect. Knowing what your triggers are will aid in understanding why you react the way you do in certain situations. The beauty of behaviors is that there is always a core reason. Not identifying your triggers sometimes can yield bad behavior and negatively impact your relationships, livelihood, and overall enjoyment of life. Imagine being in a situation where maybe a potential job is on the line through a networking opportunity, and something happens that causes you to react rudely. Now, tolerating disrespect or any unfair treatment is not acceptable. However, being mindful of your behavior is important. Our human make-up encompasses a variety of emotions; frustration, happiness, disappointment, excitement and apprehension. Our emotions relate to some event, memory or experience that you no longer have to be bound to if that's what you truly desire. You can recognize them and take charge!

So when developing effective verbal response/habits when it

comes to triggers, here are some questions to help identify triggers:

1. What does my mind and body say? (Symptoms of Anxiety)

2. Do I feel this way every time it happens, or I notice similar circumstances?

3. Have I healed from the event, experience or memory?

4. What can I do differently not to react the same when I am potentially triggered again?

Be Kind To Yourself-You Deserve It, No Matter What You May Feel In a Moment

"Be Kind To Yourself" has to be the most mind-blowing phrase that my therapist consistently stated throughout my journey. We often hear, especially as children, to be kind to others. "Do unto others as you would want others to do unto you." Well, let me speak for myself. I was always so focused on being kind to others that I was caught off guard when my therapist told me to be kind to myself. Like, wow, I can actually do that, but exactly what does that mean? It's crazy how sometimes we questioned the simplest words. When making mistakes/bad choices or not liking something about myself, I would speak to myself so badly. Whether it's calling myself fat, big and unattractive when I've put on some unwanted pounds or because I've always occupied a curvier body. Or even when I've lost the weight would always still refer to myself in such a way. And anytime I've resented the choices that I've made, my first thing and many times after is to call myself stupid. One of the worst things one person can say to themselves. Now I won't act as if I haven't talked unkindly to myself since discovering that being kind to yourself is imperative to my mental health, but I now recognize it and let myself know that it's not okay and correct myself. Unfortunately, it's a bad habit that I've been so accustomed to that it will take time and work to affirm and make this a permanent habit.

When it comes to being kind to yourself, here are ways to develop this verbal habit:

- " I am my biggest advocate."
- "I acknowledge the error I made, and I forgive myself."
- "Today I will reward myself for   ."
- "Today, I will take care of me and rest."
- "I respect myself today, tomorrow, and every day after."

- " I am strong in the area(s) of   ."
- " I will affirm myself constantly."
- "I am not perfect, and that's okay."
- "I will show myself grace."
- I believe in myself and accept who I am."

You Got Strengths and Limitations. And It's Okay

"The only limitation is that which one sets up in one's own mind"

—Napoleon Hill

I always thought my limitations, what some may know as weaknesses, made me less of a person. The enemy (our mind) will always try to convince us that because we have some limitations, that means we are incapable. Another one of my childhood dreams was to become a model. Secretly, I fell in love with modeling. I would watch America's Next Top Model for hours. Now, modeling wasn't something I thought about before watching the show. Me being a model was the furthest thing from my mind growing up. But after I started watching the show, I instantly fell in love with what seemed to be magic. The magic of getting glammed up, transforming into someone else, speaking and getting in front of the camera to bring a visual story to life. Watching this show gave me a sense of comfort, knowing that there were a lot of tall women in the world.

My height was something I always struggled with. I would be in my room, practicing posing and of course "smizing" (smiling with your eyes). I would watch this show and imagine Tyra herself was standing in front of me, calling my name to move on to the next phase. Now, you would think because I imagined it, practicing in my room and watching the show constantly, that I would have tried to pursue it. Well, no! Remember I said I secretly fell in love with modeling. I never told a soul. They all just thought I loved watching the show. But why didn't I say anything? Well, I didn't think I had what it takes to actually be a model. I thought my flat feet would hinder me. And the modeling world back then was based anywhere around a size 0, and I am far from that. While I was dreaming and practicing, I was also coming up with every reason why modeling wasn't for me or why I wasn't born to be a model.

I simply didn't believe I had what it took. I allowed my limitations to determine right off that I couldn't be a model instead of believing in my strengths and step out on faith.

Have you ever allowed your limitations to stop you from pursuing a dream? Now don't get me wrong, I don't have any regrets about not becoming a model. I truly believe I am where I'm supposed to be. But looking back, if I could tell my younger self to at least share your dreams with your parents and possibly try it just to see what happens. What I've learned throughout my journey is that how we see ourselves and what we believe is very important. The world already puts limits on us. We don't have to too. As I stated before, I've learned quite a bit about myself via therapy, and one thing for sure I discovered is that I found comfort in my limitations. To break this limiting belief of thinking, I can't achieve something solely based on my limitations. The fact of the matter is we all have limitations. It's not about having them but what we're going to do about them.

Affirm with yourself, *"I will not allow my limitations to control my mind and hinder me in any area of life"*.

Challenging Your Thoughts-Never Make the Mistake Of Thinking One Way

"Cultivation of the mind should be the ultimate aim of human

existence."

—B.R. Ambedkar

How amazing would it be if there was only one way to approach anything or how to feel about something. Limiting beliefs are heavily centered around the fact that we don't challenge our thoughts. I made the mistake of thinking that time and prayer were the only way to get through anything. Again, a clear reason as to why I prolonged starting therapy. By taking action to better my mental health, I, in turn, challenge my therapy thoughts. I, in some way, went out to see if my thoughts were true or that I didn't have a clue at all. When you are evaluating your past experiences and trying to understand the outcome, you may think that the reasoning is because of one thing, while after going through a deeper dive to understand, you uncover a completely different reason. And that reason alone adjusts your mindset and behaviors.

When you come across those moments of negative thoughts, the first word you can use to adjust is, STOP! And then challenge your thoughts by asking yourself some questions. "Why am I thinking this way? Get in company with others who would respectfully challenge your thoughts. In one of my discussions with my book coach, I mentioned that I should have taken time to heal before entering another relationship. And she challenged my thoughts to consider the fact that sometimes some people can heal by being loved properly by someone. I appreciated her challenging me to think deeper. The fact of the matter is we all play some role in someone else's healing process. That doesn't mean we could do that with any and everyone. It comes down to the right people or person at the right time.

Celebrate Your Wins- I Mean Why Not? YOU GO GIRL!

"Life is too short not to celebrate nice moments!"

—Jurgen Klopp

No one does not NOT want to win in life, right? Have you ever accomplished something big, like it was a pretty big deal for you, and you wanted to share that news with someone and didn't get the response you thought you would? Yes, me too! And did that reaction leave you hesitant to not only not share wins again but also fail to celebrate your wins yourself? Yes, me too! Therapy has helped me understand that a win is a win for me. No matter how big or small, no matter how someone else feels about it, it is a win. I also had to adjust my mindset of what wins are. Wins are not just getting that new job, selling out of your product-based business or winning the lottery. Wins can also be simply that you got out of bed after having a week of low, dark moments, it could be that you incorporated two self-care days in one month instead of just one or even that you managed to not let that specific person in your life cross a boundary that would disrupt your peace. Again, a win is a win! Be proud of yourself.

When I realized that my low moments had become less frequent, I started to celebrate that, and it would be the first thing I would mention in my therapy sessions. Letting my therapist know how great I was feeling and how my days were going. If you are someone who is currently struggling with your mental health, let me be the first to tell you, don't think for one moment that better days aren't ahead. Yes, all our situations are not the same, but things will get better as long as work is being done. Even in your lowest moments, find moments to celebrate. Oftentimes we may confuse being grateful with celebrating wins. Yes, it's imperative to be grateful. But being grateful doesn't necessarily mean you always celebrate the things you accomplish. Especially when it may seem small. But again, a win is a win. I'm going to repeat it for you and me. It's the celebration that's the vital part, not necessarily the win itself. Celebrating it only means you recognize it. It means you see yourself, and that's what is important. Don't get me wrong, the win itself is great, but you are showing yourself some love when you celebrate the win. And what's better than self-love...nothing. And I stand on that! A lot of times, when we are not doing this, we become our worst enemy. We often let the lack of celebration from others determine how we view ourselves, how worthy we are of that celebration.

We have all heard that common saying in ways, " be your own cheerleader" or " be your biggest cheerleader" some may think it's cliche, but it's true. If you don't cheer yourself on, you leave it up to others to do it and when they don't, you're left disappointed. And that disappointment then prompts you to limit what you celebrate. When we allow this type of disappointment, we allow ourselves to believe that we need to be validated by others. Don't relinquish that power, sis! I know this all too well. I always looked for my family and friends to validate me as a person based on how they felt, reacted to my wins or even how they loved me. I remember getting a promotion at work some years back and sharing it with some friends, and when that news wasn't received the way I thought, it made me want to no longer share.. It made me feel as if I was doing something wrong by sharing and it made me feel as though I needed to deem my light in that area of my life with them.

My Mantras to Celebrate Wins:

- "I have accomplished ____, and I am proud of myself."
- "I will share my wins with family and friends when I am open to sharing."
- "I will not look for anyone else to celebrate my wins."
- "I will not be disappointed when others do not celebrate my wins."
- "I will reward myself for wins, whether big or small."
- "I set a goal and will celebrate each milestone that brings me closer to my overall goal."
- "I will celebrate if no one else will."

CHAPTER 8
CREATING GENERATIONAL MENTAL WEALTH

"Even the smallest shift in perspective can bring about the greatest healing."

—Joshua Kai

ALTER YOUR PARADIGMS

What I've discovered is that I'd never healed from anything that has hurt me. I would think that I did, but actually, I just suppressed it with time and distractions. In reality, all I was doing was just piling on hurt after hurt. I didn't deal with anything because I simply didn't know how I was supposed to. I wasn't learning from any of those experiences but continuing in a bad cycle. You see, the kind of mindset we have can either make you gain swift momentum or keep you in the dark like I was. Cindy Trimm once said, "If you desire to see changes you must alter the paradigms that shapes your belief system". We don't have to continue using the same coping mechanisms generation after generation, especially if those methods aren't yielding positive results.

RECREATE AND RENEW

My seasons of pain and struggles birth my seasons to recreate and renew myself. I'm learning to forgive myself, forget the mistake and remember the lesson. Everything I'm destined to be and create is birthed from this trial, and for that, I must give thanks. I'm probably in the best place in my life, and that's discovering God's purpose for my life. Not discovering the purpose I want for myself nor the purpose anyone else wants for me. This chapter, for me, is more monumental than any other because I'm making myself and my mental health a priority.

Amid me learning how to love myself, I fell in love with all things self-care. I literally binged watch self-care routines on YouTube and started applying different aspects to my life and becoming committed to it. From reading a book to a nice hot bath, giving myself a facial, to finding a new hobby, no matter how simple it is, it's all about the fact that I am setting aside dedicated time to me, frequently. It helps bring a sense of calmness, relaxation and helps control my emotional triggers. If this is something you don't include in your life, I highly suggest it as a method for taking care of yourself. There are so many ways to pay attention to ourselves and recognize what we are needing in a specific moment. Self-care looks different for everyone, so find what soothes you.

SELF-SOOTHE- GIVE YOURSELF SOME LOVE TOO

Therapy has taught me how to recognize those things that soothe me, especially when my anxiety is high. As a corporate professional, a lot of my career has been surrounded by problem-solving. And that's how I view self-soothing methods. Now, don't get me wrong, self-soothing won't always change the result or circumstances of a situation. Having mental/emotional struggles can indeed seem like a problem; however, self-soothing can ease the problem and adjust how you handle things.

Sit In That Discomfort...You'll Never Know What's On the Other Side

We naturally want to be comfortable, we want to be at peace, and depending on the person, you may run away from conflict. And that conflict can be internal. Therapy forced me to sit in my discomfort. With having low self-esteem and not reflecting self-love, I often ran away from anything that made me uncomfortable. My therapist assigned me the homework of sitting in front of my mirror and saying everything I thought about myself, stating what I would work on forgiving myself and overall looking at myself and loving me. So, I sat down in front of my floor mirror and took on that assignment because of my commitment to doing the work. Quite naturally, it was uncomfortable and awkward in the beginning. For the first few minutes, I just sat there and looked at myself, searching for my thoughts and sitting in all my emotions. The assignment was not only to do this but also to do it multiple times and establish this as a form of self-soothing when I needed it.

I'm committed to doing something I've never done before, and that's serving the season I'm currently in. I am where I am, and that's where I must be mentally, especially regarding depression and anxiety. Depression and anxiety are a part of my story, but they aren't who I am. Therapy has helped me understand how to live and not live with them.

Meaning, I fully recognize and understand them and the triggers associated with them, however, I refuse to become a victim to them. The goal is to continue the self-work and not run away from depression and anxiety. And the true beauty of this reckoning is that I understand some days may be better than others, and that's okay, it's life, and I'm human. Therapy has taught me how to not only feel my emotions but evaluate them and how to move on to a place of peace.

It's important, now more than ever, to focus on your mental health. It's not about being perfect and living up to standards but gradually transforming into who we are destined to be. We are all influenced by some outside force, whether it's family, friends, social media or culture, whatever it may be.

If you're someone who does not want to spend the money on therapy, think about it from an investment standpoint. Therapy is just like paying for your education, paying for maintenance such as car repairs, or investing in the stock market. They are all to make your life better in some way. I, too, thought it wasn't worth it, but when I look at the things I already spend my money on, it's more than worth it. Honestly, there were things I didn't need but was spending the money to have because I wanted them. So why not invest in something that is worth it and vital to my life in every aspect. I know it's easier said than done, especially in today's economy, but try not to worry about the financial aspect of therapy or research financially sound options that would still be effective. Don't worry about what those around you will say. Just take the steps and seek therapy and make it a part of a new normal. It's a positive adjustment to your life. Every day you wake up to doing something, whether it's simply to go to work to pay bills or raise a family, look at therapy as an outlet to maintain and effectively operate in life.

GENERATIONAL IMPACT

One of the best things about life as long as you're living is that working on yourself never has to end. Anytime you expand, grow to new heights, you're only reaching areas that unlock for you to work towards even more greatness. Yes, life is short and everyday isn't promised but we can find joy in the pursuit of growth and evolution.

I want mental health to be so normalized that our kids are learning about it more in school. That not only are they going for their yearly physical check up, they also get their mental yearly check up as well.

I want mental health to be so normalized that we no longer associate it with only those with extreme behavior problems but also those who smile, laugh, socialize and excel.

When I decided to go to the hospital for my depression, it took my family completely out of their comfort zone as well as myself. My family was used to me being okay, functioning well and simply being myself. I know that my journey is not in vain. My hope is that mental health becomes so normalized that the generations ahead will never be uncomfortable, or apprehensive when they or someone else says that they are struggling with their mental health. It's not about positioning mental health as something to avoid in life but positioning it so that generations of people recognize and react in the healthiest ways possible. The goal is not to walk around wounded and damaged but to walk in the light of overcoming and encouraging someone.

Before, I was always in pursuit of creating generational financial wealth even if it's simply to learn how to save more or create additional streams of income but now I desire to pass on so much more to my children, nephews and any young person coming after me. The reality is we can't enjoy financial wealth if our mental health is not aligned as well. There's this misconception that more money brings happiness, it may definitely minimize problems to a certain extent but it's not a remedy for dealing with depression and/or anxiety, healing from trauma or removing limiting beliefs. But the fact of the matter is that generational wealth can't be sustained without mental stability because it simply won't be an easy road to obtain.

We are living in a new day where people are starting to break generational curses, habits and beliefs that hinder us long term. And by choosing not to repeat those things does not demean the generations before us but shows growth in how to live. I believe that every generation has at some point passed on something good that we like to keep passing on for years to come. But unfortunately, mental health struggles in the African American culture have been ignored and shunned for far too long. So instead of recycling toxic and traumatizing and unhealthy lifestyles, we can start passing on resources, coping mechanisms and the mindset that does not suppress emotional struggles. The big picture here is to save lives, strengthen relationships and be the best versions of ourselves. As long as we operate in the limiting belief that therapy is unnecessary, we will continue to pass on those stigmas. Why not teach those coming after us that their mental health matters. Why not show the younger generation different ways to handle life. Life is hard and there is nothing we can do to change that. But we can give those behind us the space to feel comfortable to say "I'm not okay".

CHAPTER 8
IT'S ME FOR ME

"Only I can change my life. No one can do it for me."
—Carol Burnett

Oftentimes when we find ourselves in moments of reflection on a journey of healing and overcoming, we think about the things we could have done differently or wish we could go back in time and tell ourselves the things we know now. Self-reflection is an integral part of the journey. And a very common activity for healing is writing a letter to your younger self. In this chapter, I am focusing on speaking to myself at a defining point in my life, which I've talked about during this book. I'm referring to myself at age 30. Granted, it wasn't that long ago, but if I had to choose a point in my life to go back and give myself a message, it would be 30. Before 30, I kinda thought I had it all figured out in some way. I thought that I was this mature, grown woman who was just simply living life. Although I was embarking on so much at that time, career growth and becoming a first-time homeowner, I thought anything coming after would simply just come and any emotional moments would subside. Not knowing that I didn't in fact have it all figured out.

Hey, girl, hey (this is how I greet my good girlfriends),

Let me start by saying you are worth more than you think. You are embarking on this next chapter of your life that's going to be a doozy sometimes. You thought your 20s was something else,.Nah sis. Your 30s will be on a whole other level and guess what, you're going to survive and thrive. It's okay that at 30 you don't have it all. And by all means, everything you hope to have. Somethings won't work out the way you want them to, and it's okay to be sad and upset, but you will move past it. One thing is for sure, I can't go back in time and prevent anything bad from happening, and I can't make the things you want magically appear. However, I will tell you that you are pretty strong and a true fighter. Stronger and tougher than you think! You're not that same little girl you once were. You no longer have to carry her hand and protect her. You've walked beside her long enough. You no longer have to defend who she was because she no longer exists. Yes, the heart and soul of her is still there and will forever be, but you have grown past her. And you can now start living for you. Let go of her hand and be who you are now.

Yes, as I said, you are strong, but you also don't have to walk in the spirit of emotional avoidance. There is strength in being vulnerable. It's okay to live outside your mind and feelings. That's the beauty of being you and being a human. You're going to go through some ugly, dark phases but yet there will be moments of beauty and light. Oh, did I tell you that you are beautiful? Yes, you're beautiful inside and out. You no longer have to be uncomfortable when receiving compliments. You've felt this uncomfortableness for 30 years, and it's time you get comfortable with God's creation, YOU! You no longer have to limit the amount of time you look into the mirror or even avoid looking at yourself altogether. Find the beauty in every curve and every flaw. It's okay to want to work on things but always, always do them for YOU! And stop comparing yourself to the next person! Don't allow a man's choice to define how you view yourself. Someone not choosing you is God's protection. Their loss Sis!

Oh, did I mention you're enough! This is something you have forever struggled with, and it's time you struggle no more.

You don't have to question this no matter what may transpire in your life or no matter what someone who says it or shows it through their actions. Stop always focusing on areas of lack and celebrate your fulfilled areas. You're going to learn more and more on how not to allow titles nor possessions to define who you are. Becoming a wife and mother are true blessings but do not determine your value and the reason for your existence. Don't allow society's timeline of life to get to you. God says you're right on time.

Oh, and don't let me forget to tell you to forgive yourself. Give yourself grace for who you were in those moments of choice. Take accountability and then work through those moments where regret arises. You've always tried to see the good in people because you're so focused on filling positions in your life because you think that's what you're supposed to do. Trust that God will send the right people and remove those who no longer serve the season that you're in. You may have confused physical connection and words with unconditional love and that's just the lesson you've learned.

Let me tell you one thing, Sis, you will evolve into multiple versions of who you are. You are going to be amazed at the *woman you become in your 30s. That's right. I said WOMAN. You will grow out of that "woman-girl" mentality and walk in growth, evolution and maturity; however, note I didn't say perfection. Yes, you no longer have to always strive for perfection. Yes, it's okay to have a work ethic that produces good work and a sense of creating quality standards. But trying to be perfect in every way will lead you to multiple moments of dissatisfaction. Live and don't minimize your existence.*

I challenge you to reflect and write a letter to yourself at any defining point in your life. Whether that's you as a child, in college or maybe just a year ago, it's up to you. What therapy has taught me is how to reflect and speak to myself in multiple ways. Whether standing in the mirror and having a full-on conversation with myself or simply journaling to release what's on the inside.

A BETTER ME FOR THE FUTURE

Therapy has altered who I am in the future. In life, our roles and positions may change, we may take on new titles or leave some behind. For me, I recognize that therapy gives me a better shot of fulfilling those roles effectively and to break generational curses. Therapy has allowed me to heal and equip myself with more knowledge and wisdom to be a better professional, business woman, daughter, sister, aunt, friend, and future wife and mother. Again, doesn't mean I will always get it right, but I will be able to recognize and correct it. I healed so that my future children won't have to heal from my trauma. I learned new ways to live so that my children will find normalcy in vulnerability. I altered my perception of life so that I could learn to show up differently in my relationships with others. I educated myself on the complexities of the mind and normalized diversified methods of treatment.

ABOUT THE AUTHOR

Kelsey Brewster is a corporate professional with years of experience in problem-solving, leadership and driving for results. She has fulfilled a childhood dream of becoming an author. In Nobody Understands Me But My Therapist, Kelsey talks about her journey with mental health, taking charge of her depression and anxiety, discovering clinical talk therapy and finding the confidence and courage to share with others in hopes that they too will take action when it comes to their mental health.

Nobody Understands Me But My Therapist

NORMALIZING THERAPY WHEN DEPRESSION,
ANXIETY & LIMITING BELIEFS ARE REAL

Subscribe Today

Stay connected for all upcoming events and updates.
Visit kelseybrewster.com

@iamkelseyb | www.kelseybrewster.com

References:

- CDC: (Introduction, page 16-17)
- Charlamagne the God Book: https://www.amazon.com/Shook-One-Anxiety-Playing-Tricks/dp/1501193252 (Chapter 3, pg 42) *this was that 2 that was stuck in his name that I said to remove but it was the reference)
- Power-Tv Guide link: (Chapter 4 page 54)
- Health.havard.edu/topics/depression (Chapter 5, page 70)
- Heathline.com/health/depression (Chapter 5, page 70)
- Https://www.healthline.com/health/anxiety-symptoms (Chapter 5, page 70)
- "Living Single episode https://www.tvguide.com/tvshows/living-single/episodes-season-3/1000131819/ (Chapter 5, 72/ Chapter 6, page 90)

www.ingramcontent.com/pod-product-compliance
Lightning Source LLC
Chambersburg PA
CBHW050734030426
42336CB00012B/1556